Tips For Coping With Misophonia

Anish .N Holding

Introduction

This book provides an in-depth exploration of misophonia, a condition characterized by strong emotional reactions to specific sounds. The guide begins by defining misophonia and debunking common misconceptions, emphasizing the legitimacy of trigger sounds and extending the discussion to include visual triggers.

Examining the factors influencing misophonia, such as age of onset, gender, genetics, and co-occurring disorders, the guide sets the stage for an interdisciplinary treatment approach. It advocates for collaboration among various healthcare professionals, including primary health doctors, neurologists, audiologists, occupational therapists, individual therapists, psychiatrists, and family therapists.

The guide delves into the neurophysiological aspects of misophonia, exploring the role of the sympathetic and parasympathetic nervous systems, as well as the concepts of arousal and valence. It introduces the Relaxation, Relationship, and Rhythmicity (RRR) principles, emphasizing their application in sensory strategies to manage misophonic reactions.

Practical strategies are presented for keeping arousal low, incorporating relaxing activities and everyday practices. Examples include outdoor walks, designated spaces in the house, and listening to music. The guide also introduces translational activities and resetting techniques, weaving these approaches together for a holistic self-regulation framework.

A significant portion of the guide is dedicated to helping clinicians assist clients in understanding and visualizing the fight-or-flight response associated with misophonia. Tools for tracking triggers, separating physiological and emotional responses, and monitoring habituation are provided, along with worksheets and reminder sheets.

In addressing challenges, the guide explores options such as movement, trigger avoidance, and family dynamics, offering nuanced strategies for both children and adults. Couple negotiations, the determination of necessary and unnecessary sounds, and the use of worksheets to enhance communication are also covered.

The guide concludes by addressing potential concerns when self-regulation strategies may not work, highlighting alternative approaches and reinforcing the importance of ongoing support and understanding for individuals with misophonia.

Contents

1.
Defining Misophonia

The Dominos of Disbelief

To thoroughly understand a new disorder, it helps to review its history. Without attention to its history, the medical community often regards a newly proposed condition as unreal because descriptions have been haphazardly built out of ambiguous bits of information that ultimately don't add up to anything grounded in theory. Until recently, almost every academic or popular press article about misophonia began like this:

"Misophonia, which means hatred of sound, was termed by Jastreboff and Jastreboff in 2001."

After this cursory mention of the Jastreboffs and their role in naming misophonia, authors often jump to their own interpretations. Misophonia has, unfortunately, fallen victim to this phenomenon, which I call "the dominos of disbelief."

To help put together the puzzle pieces of misophonia, let's review the original conception of the disorder. While working in their audiology clinic, the Jastreboffs observed that some people reacted to sounds such as chewing, pencil tapping, keyboard typing, and coughing with levels of irritability ranging from moderate to extreme (Brout et al., 2018).

Unlike their patients with *hyperacusis*, a disorder in which people perceive sounds more loudly than objectively measured, the Jastreboffs noticed that individuals with misophonia appeared to respond to pattern-based sounds with autonomic nervous system arousal. That is, upon presentation of such stimuli, patients reported rising stress levels such as elevated heartbeat, muscle tension, and sweating along with strong, negative emotions. This was different from what the Jastreboffs had seen regarding other forms of "decreased sound tolerance" (Jastreboff & Jastreboff, 2001) such as *tinnitus,* which is the ringing in one or both ears, and *phonophobia*, which is the fear of sound often secondary to hyperacusis.

Taking this a step back, think about how to conceptualize misophonia based on its origins. Although the Jastreboffs suggested that misophonia involves negative associations between auditory, cognitive, and emotional areas of the brain, they did not view misophonia as a *psychiatric disorder* (personal communication, 2015). In the past few years, research has clarified that misophonia is a disorder that crosses the boundaries of disciplines (Brout et al., 2018). For this reason, coping skills are based on multidisciplinary research and treatment and take into consideration movement to self-regulate.

What is a Trigger Sound?

The sounds that the misophonic find highly aversive are known as *trigger sounds*. Across early studies, symptoms reported by individuals with misophonia varied. Also, across studies, there was a striking similarity between the sounds typically considered triggering. While Jastreboff and Jastreboff (2001) mentioned “pattern-based sounds,” repetitive sounds are also an issue (Brout et al., 2018). Notably, the Jastreboffs (2001) did not suggest that these sounds were primarily mouth sounds or even necessarily generated by other human beings. Yet, Kumar et al.’s (2021) paper, in which the orofacial motor cortices are involved, supports the idea that people/mouth sounds may be more severe triggers for those with misophonia. However, we must keep in mind that many people also report difficulty with nonorganic sounds such as windshield wipers, car turn signals, and keyboard or pencil tapping (Brout et al., 2018). We await further research to clarify these confounding issues.

It is most important to inform your clients that triggers are not *contagious*. Many people have expressed this concern to me (parents, children, and adults alike). That is, people often worry that talking about triggers will result in a worsening of reactivity — or hearing about triggers will result in an increase in the number of triggering sounds. This does not seem to be true. Anecdotally, triggers seem to increase during a short period of time after the individual initially becomes aware of misophonia.

Similarly, misophonia waxes and wanes. When a client isn’t feeling well or is poorly rested, misophonia reactivity may become worse. Yet, it will likely go back to baseline when the client feels better. Try to reassure the client that they need not panic if they are going through a period of higher reactivity. Employ means to help them lessen the stressors that may be contributing to misophonia.

For this same reason, it is best not to focus on trigger sounds as separate entities but to instead focus on how the client reacts to triggers and how you can help them self-regulate. Especially considering Kumar et al.’s (2021) research that shows the motor cortex is involved in misophonia, focusing on the trigger sounds rather than how to de-escalate the neurophysiological response may not be prudent. Rather, focus on self-regulation.

What About Visual Triggers?

Schröder et al. (2013) suggested the term *misokinesia* to describe a phenomenon in which individuals experience an aversive response to repetitive visual stimuli or movement. For example, the sight of another person jiggling their leg, a common nervous habit, is frequently reported as a trigger. In view of Dr. Kumar's et al.'s (2021) work, we can see how misokinesia, as "hatred of movement," makes sense. If I see a person shaking their leg and I feel compelled to shake my leg, it is a very uncomfortable sensation that could easily make me feel a loss of physical agency. Notably, Kumar's et al.'s (2021) paper describes findings related to the orofacial motor cortex, whereas Schröder's description, as well as clinical observation, suggest other motor areas (e.g., gross motor areas may be involved). Again, we await more research to vet this out.

In sum, while the original meaning of misokinesia refers to aversive reactivity to another person's movement, many use the term to refer to any visual stimulus that causes negative reactivity. It is possible that there are two kinds of visual triggers here — one related to another person's movement, or misokinesia, and another related to memory association. That is, sounds may pair with visual stimuli in memory, thereby activating the same nervous system response.

Age of Onset

The age of onset of misophonia has been popularized in the press and reported in early academic research as occurring between 8 and 12 years of age. Yet, I have seen toddlers display symptoms. Unfortunately, research in young children regarding misophonia is just beginning. This leaves us at a loss in terms of diagnosis of these youngsters until we see the results of these studies.

Gender

Initial case studies (e.g. Bernstein et al., 2013; Ferreira et al., 2013; Johnson et al., 2013; Kluckow et al., 2014; Neal & Cavanna, 2012; Webber et al., 2014) suggest that misophonia tends to occur at a higher rate in female compared to male individuals. However, one should not make presumptions based on this early data as there may be other factors affecting this observation. For example, females have traditionally been more likely to seek help for medical and mental health–related issues than males. This finding may skew the gender ratio in Misophonia toward females.

Genetics

There has been one association of genes and misophonia. The company *23andMe* identified one genetic marker associated with misophonia (i.e., rage associated with chewing). This genetic marker is located near the TENM2 gene, which is involved in brain development. The genetic marker associated with this trait is just one piece of the puzzle and does not mean that nongenetic factors do not also play a role (Center for Disease Control, 2020). When clients ask about genetics, it is helpful to explain that geneticists think beyond the binary nature-versus-nurture terms. Instead, genes are "turned on or turned off" based on environmental events. Thus, geneticists now think in terms of nature *via* nurture (Pizzi, 2004). The study of the process by which certain genes can be turned on within individuals is called *epigenetics*. Likely then, misophonia is a combination of genetic and environmental influences. However, when clients ask, we must be careful to explain that in misophonia, we are without genetic studies at this time.

Co-Occurring Disorders

Misophonia is most likely a distinct disorder that is not better explained by the symptoms of any other disorder. However, the symptoms of misophonia are associated with other disorders and may also co-occur with other conditions. Distinct differences exist between co-occurrences and symptom overlaps. When disorders co-occur, this means that an individual meets the criterion for one or more disorders. When symptoms overlap, the individual usually meets the criterion for one disorder and not a second, yet the individual still has symptoms of both. Even though you may understand this, it is still important to explain this differential to clients as many remain confused by early reports about misophonia and its relationship to other disorders.

Both anecdotal observations and empirical findings in the audiology field suggest that there is a higher incidence of misophonia among individuals with tinnitus and/or hyperacusis (Baguley et al., 2016). In the mental health realm, misophonia and its symptoms co-occur with anxiety, obsessive-compulsive personality disorder (OCPD), sensory processing disorder (SPD), and autistic spectrum disorder (ASD). However, these co-occurrences and symptom overlaps must be viewed with caution. There is a long way to go before any of these co-occurrences or overlaps are confirmed and understood scientifically. Yet, these possibilities are important to keep in mind due to their implications for a client's experience of misophonia, diagnosis, and coping-skills development. These overlaps and co-occurrences are also one of the best justifications for multidisciplinary research, diagnosis, and treatment.

Summary

As is true of most newly termed disorders, early studies can be misleading as researchers begin with hypotheses. Early research is often not funded, and therefore, only small samples or case studies are possible. Regarding misophonia, the press picked up on some misinformation quite early, making for a highly confusing picture of what the disorder is. Over the past 5 years, more stringent research has come into play, and we can more easily identify some of the common myths.

Misophonia is not simply rage in response to chewing. As the Jastreboffs originally suggested, adverse reactivity occurs in response to a variety of patterned-based sounds—some people-centric, others nonorganic. Misophonia may co-occur with other auditory, psychological, and possibly health-related disorders, but it is not considered a psychiatric or personality disorder. The relationship of age and gender to misophonia is still anecdotal, and genetic work is in the very early stages. However, research is ongoing, and you can reassure clients that answers are forthcoming.

In the next section, I discuss how to help clients by leading or involving a multi-disciplinary team. Since this is a book for a variety of clinicians, I will outline briefly how each discipline can support those with misophonia. It is also important to remember the kinds of characteristics those with misophonia tend to seek out in therapists. Willingness to either case manage or to assist clients in doing so is most essential as clients usually end up managing their own (or their child's) treatment.

2.
Interdisciplinary Treatment

Many of us are independent practitioners and working in an interdisciplinary manner is not easy. It is time consuming and sometimes requires unpaid hours. However, it can make or break your success as a clinician working with misophonia clients. People with misophonia may begin by asking their primary doctors for help and parents may begin seeking help from their pediatricians. Many with misophonia symptoms seek out audiologists, psychologists, counselors, and sometimes occupational therapists. Since there is no recommended protocol for misophonia treatment, it is unpredictable as to where one may seek help. Regardless of what kind of practitioner you are, there are always ways you can assist clients in helping manage an interdisciplinary team even if you are not able to be the case manager yourself.

Case Management

Too many individuals end up struggling to manage their own

care or that of their child's. It is very helpful to remember that while doing this, they also inadvertently open themselves up to criticism. Parents are often referred to as *pushy or annoying.* Adults with misophonia are often told they are imagining their symptoms and have a disorder that "doesn't exist." I experienced this despite being a psychologist, and it was both painful and frustrating.

Although there is no elixir for this, there are steps you can take to minimize the impact of these experiences on clients. Try not to be judgmental. Let the client explain their experience of misophonia to you. Remember, none of us are misophonia experts although some practitioners claim to be. Please don't be that practitioner. Admit what you know and what you don't and understand that you may be learning from your client. Remember that individuals with misophonia have often been rebuffed and/or involved with unsuccessful treatments. Along with research and consultation with other clinicians, authenticity with clients is essential.

Of course, you want to reassure your client that you have done your research and understand misophonia. However, it is best to position yourself as supportive and as willing to continue to learn as research unfolds. Naturally, people with this disorder want to hear that there is a *quick fix*. However, there isn't one, and false claims to that nature are more harmful than helpful.
The following is a list of multidisciplinary professionals you may consider working with and/or referring out to depending on your area of specialty:

Primary Health Doctors & Neurologists

Research in terms of misophonia and medical disorders is very sparse, but it is always beneficial to make sure your client is up to date on their yearly physical exam. In addition, the primary doctor may refer to a neurologist. One of the most problematic issues I have heard regarding primary medical doctors is that they have never heard of misophonia and thus don't know what symptoms to look for in terms of ruling out other disorders. If a client finds themselves in this situation, reaching out to the medical professional and providing recent research or a literature review is helpful. Providing clients with information to approach these medical professionals will help them as well. However, it is important that you don't rely on a client or medical professionals to do this work. While we would like to think medical professionals are able, they are often short on time and simply don't believe in newly termed disorders. At the end of this book, you will find a list of references a client may give to medical professionals or that you can share directly with other clinicians. The "References" section of this book is a resource in its own right.

Audiologists

Audiologists assist individuals with misophonia by introducing sound generators or special apps to mask certain sounds and/or generate white noise or other kinds of noises based on frequency. Devices such as these may mask trigger sounds while still allowing the individual to hear and participate in conversations. With these devices, audiologists may provide individuals the means to reduce their sensitivity to aversive sounds. I always suggest seeing an audiologist first or an *ear–nose–throat (ENT) doctor* to rule out any anatomical issues with the ear or other auditory disorders. As we take the recent work by Kumar et al., (2021) regarding the mirror neuron hypothesis (motor basis of misophonia) into consideration, we understand that while the auditory system may not provide the entire answer to our understanding of misophonia, it is still one of the conduits to sympathetic nervous system arousal. Therefore, I feel that an audiological screening is imperative to rule out other audiological problems.

Occupational Therapists (OTs)

Physiological or sensory-based occupational therapies are those that directly affect the nervous system. A simple breathing technique is a form of physiological therapy. Occupational therapists (OTs) are specially trained to work with the sensory systems that are intertwined with the nervous system. They are also excellent clinicians when it comes to working with children with numerous disorders that include self-regulation difficulties. There are some general ways that help people self-regulate. Yet, each person is an individual in the specific ways sensation may be used to assist calming the system, and OTs are unique in their training to do this.

While OTs provide perhaps some of the best methods for physiological self-regulation, they also sometimes suggest Listening Therapy Programs. These programs were not devised for people with misophonia and have not been properly researched for those with misophonia. Should an OT suggest this or want to use this, please make sure the clients know this is experimental. For more information on listening therapies see: https://sensoryhealth.org/search/node?keys=Listening+Therapy

Individual Therapists and Counselors

Individual therapy and supportive counseling can be beneficial for anyone in distress. As you likely know, psychologists and counselors have many different approaches and work from various schools of thought. The theoretical grounding and different types of therapists and counselors available is extensive. This is often overwhelming to people seeking help. In regard to misophonia, it is crucial that you take it upon yourself to explain your background, your therapeutic framework, and how you intend to help.

For example, and as you may know, Cognitive Behavior Therapy (or CBT) is used very generally while the term encompasses many different interventions. It is best not to take for granted that your client knows there are different CBT interventions. Part of your job as a *misophonia therapist or counselor* is to explain how and what you do will help but also what limitations exist. For a comprehensive list of CBTs, see www.infocounselling.com/list-of-cbt-techniques.

Finally, according to the American Psychological Association (2017), exposure therapy has been utilized successfully for anxiety, obsessive compulsive and related disorders, as well as post-traumatic stress disorder and phobias. Exposure therapy is not a validated treatment for misophonia. Many psychologists have turned to this form of treatment, specifically graded exposure therapy in which the therapist begins with mild exposures and then moves towards more difficult exposures. The goal of exposure therapy is to systematically desensitize the individual to the stimuli or stimulus. There is little to no evidence that this works for misophonia, and most clients report high levels of discomfort. Individuals also report that they do not desensitize (or habituate) to the sounds/visuals.

Psychiatrists

While there is no medically approved treatment for misophonia, psychiatrists may assist in parsing out and treating comorbid conditions. It is helpful to address comorbid conditions, if possible, therefore making it easier for the patient to cope with misophonia.

Psychiatrists may also suggest treating symptoms by using off-label medications for their misophonic patients. It is imperative for any medical doctor to explain their rationale for doing so, and make sure the patient knows that this is experimental (and, of course, understands the risks). There have been no studies regarding misophonia and medication currently.

Couples and Family Therapists

When we are dealing with a child or an adult with misophonia, the entire family and couple dynamic is impacted. Given that, couples and family therapists can be of great value in the face of these specific challenges (Shadish & Baldwin, 2003). Regarding the family, there are numerous schools of thought in terms of practicing family therapy. I find that a family systems approach is best for misophonia.

Psychiatrist Murray Bowen, M.D. was one of the pioneers of family systems therapy. Dr. Bowen noted that positive changes in one family member changed the way everyone else functioned (The Bowen Center for the Study of the Family, n.d.). The changes that took place did not necessarily occur first within the family member identified as the patient. Considering this observation, Dr. Bowen maintained that the family, not the patient, should be the focus of treatment.

The value of the systems approach is that when one person in the family makes a positive change, even if it is not the identified patient, the system changes for the better. Unfortunately, many family therapists who could be of tremendous value in misophonia management as a sub-discipline have not yet become as familiar with misophonia, and we need them aboard. As a case manager or as the clinician helping with case management, please reach out, consult, and share resources with these practitioners.

Biofeedback Practitioners

These practitioners use biofeedback along with guided imagery and other relaxation techniques or distractive methods to affect physiological change. During a biofeedback session, one can see their stress responses on a monitor in real time and may use various cognitive and physiologically based relaxation techniques to learn how to improve reactivity to triggers.

While some people have found biofeedback helpful, few studies show significant and/or lasting change. Another issue with biofeedback is that it may be difficult for the individual to transfer what they have learned during biofeedback sessions into a moment of misophonic responding. Biofeedback can be helpful as an adjunct to other coping skills methods, yet there is no evidence that biofeedback is, on its own, a form of therapy for misophonia. Unfortunately, it has been touted as such, and we must be careful to inform clients of its benefits and limitations.

Neurofeedback Practitioners

This technique is like biofeedback. However, rather than attaching sensors to the body to monitor heart rate, *electroencephalogram (EEG)* sensors are attached to the scalp to monitor brain activities. In a neurofeedback practitioners office, one may see their brain waves appear on a monitor in the form of a game. The goal is to alter one's brain waves to a more adaptive pattern. Again, it is up to the individual to use physiological and cognitive skills to affect change. Notably, brain waves are only one small facet of understanding the exceedingly complex functioning of the brain. Again, biofeedback and neurofeedback can certainly be helpful as part of a multidisciplinary coping skills plan. However, there is no evidence that either are a validated treated for misophonia.

Summary

It can be frustrating for the client to figure out who to turn to for help, which is why RRR integrates skill training across disciplines. From my experience, coping skills training works well when a clinician is willing to be a partner in this process and not the *authority*. I say this again because none of us are misophonia authorities at this time. The following is a list of practitioner traits that I feel are most important for effective treatment:

- Knowledge of misophonia and/or willingness to learn about misophonia from professional workshops, forums, and peer-reviewed papers.

- A willingness to reach out to multi-disciplinary practitioners and be the case manager if necessary.
- Flexibility. Since we are in new territory with misophonia, flexibility is highly important. If something you are doing is not working or is negatively impacting your client, it is imperative that you address this and find other ways to proceed or make a referral to another clinician. Of course, reaching out to other professionals for consultation is also an excellent option.

While much of this may seem obvious to you, it is important to take extra care as those with misophonia have often been dismissed by clinicians and/or treated with inappropriate interventions.

As we move into the next section, we will dig deeper into how misophonia affects the client's functioning. A review of the basics of the nervous system will help you to understand what a client is up against and how to assist toward better self-regulation. This next section may be a review for some. However, you may pick up some nuances in relation to misophonia that you may not have thought about. For others, these ideas may engender a paradigm shift.

3.

Reviewing the Neurophysiological

Understanding neurophysiological systems will allow you to better understand your clients' behavior and better promote self-regulation. In addition, reviewing the mechanisms that underlie misophonia to explain them clearly to clients is important. Any newly termed disorder is difficult to understand as misophonia is a disorder that also engenders a high level of frustration for sufferers. Although this text has referenced the nervous system generally, we are now specifically focusing on the *autonomic nervous system (ANS)*.

The ANS is one major part of the nervous system that controls the involuntary response of many organs and muscles. In most situations, we are unaware of the ANS' functioning because its actions are unconscious, thereby requiring no thought or effort (Low, 2020). The ANS contains the sympathetic, *parasympathetic,* and *enteric nervous system*. For the purposes of misophonia, we will concentrate on the sympathetic and parasympathetic nervous system.[1]

The Sympathetic Nervous System

One of the sympathetic nervous system's primary functions is to stimulate the body's fight–flight response. This physiological reaction occurs when one perceives a threat. The defense response, which is an updated term inclusive of the fight–flight reaction, enables one to fight or to escape a dire situation quickly by flooding the body with hormones that provide increased energy (Low, 2020). Even though the terms "sympathetic nervous system arousal" and "fight–flight" are used interchangeably in this text, it is important to take a moment to point out how they are different. Sympathetic arousal refers to an escalation of the sympathetic nervous system, and fight–flight is the extreme end of this escalation.

The defense response can sometimes be activated when it is not needed in situations that mimic threat by cognitively motivated fears or phobias (Ledoux, 2003). *I am worried about school grades* (thought), and my sympathetic system is activated. *I fear spiders*, thus, when I see one, I experience sympathetic system changes.

Sympathetic arousal in response to worry or anxiety may be stimulated by internal stimuli such as thoughts. In misophonia, sympathetic arousal begins directly because of outside stimuli. That is, a sound or a visual stimulus from the outside world kicks off the defense response. This is a very important distinction, setting misophonia apart from other disorders that one might consider more psychological in nature. This is very important to share with clients. It can help clients distinguish when a sound/visual is activating versus when anxiety about triggers (anticipatory anxiety) is at play.

The Parasympathetic Nervous System

The body's attempt to combat this reaction and return to homeostasis or calm involves the other part of the ANS. The parasympathetic nervous system puts on the brakes to return the body to homeostasis or neutral (Low, 2020). This is called *habituation*. Habituation is highly intertwined with self-regulation. *See table 1 below:*

Sympathetic	**Parasympathetic**
System known to be responsible for arousal that leads to fight–flight response	Puts the brakes on fight–flight response (also known as the "digest and rest" system)
Automatically set into action when outside stimuli cue that the organism may be under threat	Set into action when person has reached safety or assesses situation danger to be false
Adrenaline released and blood flow directed to major muscles	Acetylcholine released
Blood pressure increases	Lowers blood pressure and aids digestion
Heart rate increases	Heart rate decreases

Table 1. The Autonomic Nervous System (sympathetic and parasympathetic)

Alerting, Arousal, and Attention

The brain's innate ability to alert us to auditory and other sensory stimuli is essential to survival. Prior to experiencing nervous system arousal, we must be alert to stimuli. Think how we rely on our sense of smell to alert us to the potential danger of something. For example, we smell something burning and we think, "fire."

Alerting often occurs outside of, or before, the individual's awareness. Unbeknownst to us, the is brain is always scanning surroundings via our senses to know when and where to focus attention. This is known as *pre-attention*. Pre-attention, then, is not something we control. Rather, it is an unconscious process preserved by evolution that allows us to know when we are in danger (LeDoux, 2015).

Many parents have asked me why their child stares at triggering sounds or visuals. Similarly, many adults have asked me why they feel compelled to stare at what is triggering them. This is pre-attention at work. The most useful way to override our brain's natural attentional processes is to focus on one's physiological response and gain insight into how one's body reacts to sympathetic nervous system arousal. Simply suggesting to clients that they focus on something else while triggered is not enough because they are fighting their brain's natural response. It certainly helps to share this knowledge with a client or the client's parents.

Once the individual is alerted to a trigger stimulus, sympathetic nervous system arousal will occur. How can we help our clients understand what is happening to them during a misophonic response?[2] Sympathetic nervous system arousal can range from very low to very high. We've all been in low arousal states and high arousal states as well as everything in between. Here is an exercise that is very simple to do with your clients, especially older adolescents and adults. It is also helpful to ask parents to do this so that they understand their child's reactivity better.

For a moment, don't think about your emotions or thoughts. Just think about yourself in terms of your physical state. What are you doing, and how does your body feel right now? Are you reading in bed? Are you sitting up in a chair? Is your heart rate fast or normal? Are you falling asleep? Would you say your body state is calm and alert, or are you distracted?

Again, we are helping clients parse out the neurophysiological from the cognitive and emotional. You may also want to further explain that conceptually, arousal stands on its own and describes the *intensity* of a response. However, to truly make sense of one's physiological state, one must also think about *valence*, which is the qualifier for arousal. For example, I have had people ask me what the difference between dancing happily around a room (high arousal) and wanting to, for example, throw a pillow across the room (high arousal in response to misophonia trigger) is.

Reviewing the Difference between Arousal and Valence?

The terms arousal and valence describe two separate states of mind and body. Valence tells us if one's arousal level, whatever the intensity, is positive or negative. The important idea to remember is that arousal can be high when valence is low and vice versa. This is usually simple to explain to adolescents and adults but may involve more concrete work with children. For a visual representation to share with clients, see *Table 2 below.*

Arousal	Valence	Result
High	Positive	Happy, excited
Low	Negative	Depressed, sad, bored
High	Negative	Frightened, anxious, angry
Low	Positive	Calm, complacent, satisfied, relaxed

Table 2. *Arousal and Valence*

Summary

Children, adolescents, and adults with misophonia experience high arousal coupled with negative valence intermittently throughout each day and are subjected to continual dysregulation. Again, the main tenet of RRR is to address dysregulation by teaching self-regulation skills so that our clients can de-escalate the sympathetic system and better manage cognition and emotions. We can do this via practical measures as well as by teaching reliable techniques using physiologically and sensory based skills. As a reminder, Occupational Therapists (OT's) are highly skilled at this. If you are a mental health clinician, working alongside an OT is often highly beneficial to clients.

4.
Applying RRR Principles/Sensory Strategies

As we go through the next sections, we will apply the specific principles of RRR, including the use of sensory-based and other physiological strategies. We will then discuss how to integrate cognitive and practical strategies in the following sections. Yet, we will begin with the sensory–physiological because we abide by the idea of physiological regulating first. In addition, we will cover strategies that can assist with the stressors misophonia causes within the family. I provide worksheets presented in example form, and you will find the full worksheets, as well as reminders sheets, at the end of the manual.

Be Sensible (Reminder Sheet A)

We all know that certain activities are naturally calming. Some of these activities refer to what we do with babies (i.e., rocking, swaddling, patting the baby gently on the back, etc.). We may refer to these as sensory-based activities as they focus on ways to use the individuals' sensory preferences to self-regulate.

Most of us know that we have the following five senses:

- **Sight** (Vision)
- **Hearing** (Auditory)
- **Smell** (Olfactory)
- **Taste** (Gustatory)
- **Touch** (Tactile)

However, the classic list of senses continues past common knowledge and includes the following three often-overlooked senses:

- **Interoception** (what we feel inside our bodies)
- **Vestibular** (sense of balance and rotation)
- **Proprioception** (sense of where our bodies are in space, understood through input to our muscles and joints)

Interoception is the intensity with which we feel our body's internal functions. Since we know that Kumar et al. (2017) found differences in the interoceptive sense in individuals with misophonia, it follows that we include this in our investigation of our client's perception of the world.

Next, the *vestibular* sense is related to balance and body rotation. The connection between the vestibular sense and misophonia has not been established but is also worth exploring because the vestibular sense is connected to the middle ear. In fact, the vestibular sense resides in sense organs called cilia, which are little hairs deep within the ear that send out signals to the auditory nerve (Mailloux & Smith, 2013).

Finally, we must also consider the sense of *proprioception.* Proprioception tells us how and where our bodies are in space by using external sensory input to our muscles and joints. Many people find proprioceptive input to be quickly and intensely calming. Think, for example, of how many people enjoy yoga, stretching, and massage—all proprioceptive activities.

Why Use Calming Sensory-Based Activities?

There are three ways to use sensory-based activities for misophonia management. The first is to keep general sympathetic system arousal low during everyday life. These activities are important for clients to incorporate into their daily schedules. The second is to guide your client to use calming activities to bring down arousal when a client is going into a triggering situation. These activities are generally the same as the everyday ones, however, they are being used proactively. The third is to translate these activities into ones that may be used in the *misophonia moment*.

Although none of these activities are a panacea for misophonia, having them in a toolbox will help assist a client toward better self-regulation. Depending on a clients' age and developmental stage, you can rely upon an occupational therapist to assist with these activities and/or guide a client toward doing them independently.

Many adults have often found their own way of keeping their arousal levels low. Adults take walks, enjoy baths, or utilize various forms of exercise. However, it is still important to make sure that adult clients are aware of what is working and what may not be. Since all individuals are different, this may take some guided research with a client. You may ask them to track how they feel physiologically after particular experiences.

Often, with young children, it is integral that parents help their child for a while before self-regulation occurs. Remember, young children and older children with misophonia still rely on parents and other adults for physiological calming. What one may see as oppositional behavior is likely to be the inability to self-regulate. This may shift how you would normally view the parent/child interaction, and it is important that clients and parents of clients understand this as well. Historically it has been easier to find sensory information for children, and this is not an exhaustive list. However, for more information, see the STAR Institute at sensoryhealth.org.

Keeping Arousal Low (Relaxing Activities and Everyday Practice)

We know, for example, that taking a bath is calming for many of us. While bathing, we are using our tactile sense (touch) as we feel the warm water against our skin. We are also enjoying proprioceptive input (to our muscles and joints) as the pressure of the water surrounds us. Similarly, many of us find rocking chairs soothing. Rocking is a utilization of the vestibular sense, de-escalating sympathetic nervous system reactivity. It's no wonder new parents use rockers and gliders to calm their infants. Similarly, swaddling, as a parent might do with an infant, calls upon the proprioceptive sense as a baby enjoys pressure into the muscles and joints. The following list shows activities that most individuals, regardless of age, find naturally relaxing. After the list is an explanation of how the sensory system is utilized so that you can help parents or adults translate these ideas to their lives.

Keeping Arousal Low at Home: Relaxing Activities/Everyday Practice (Worksheet #1)
Massage (foot rollers, hand rollers, etc.)
Rocking (or gliding) in chair
Rocking (or gliding) in chair with weighted blanket
Rolling on the floor or mat
Stretching
Taking a bath
Weighted blanket
Yoga

Massage: Most of us understand the relaxing quality of massage. The art of massage has been around for centuries and offers pain relief. There are even massage therapists who specialize in infant massage. However, on a more practical basis, we can use foot rollers, foam rollers, scalp massagers, and the like, which are all easily found online and at sporting goods store. Again, we are using proprioceptive input (input to the muscles and joints) to bring in the parasympathetic system.

***Rocking or gliding*:** Some individuals prefer rocking and others prefer gliding. Each uses the vestibular sense to bring in the parasympathetic system and can help the individual self-regulate. Many adults can probably relate to or have even experienced how rocking or gliding is physiologically soothing to a baby or to the self. Again, regardless of age, these sensory-based principles are the same.

***Weighted blanket*:** A weighted blanket uses the sense of proprioception to calm the nervous system. The amount of weight that a person needs to calm varies (Miller et al., 2009). It is okay to experiment with different weights with your client. Should the client choose, rather than purchase an expensive weighted blanket, they can use heavy quilts and bedspreads instead. Combining the use of a weighted blanket and a rocker–glider is often very effective.

Stretching: Stretching also provides input to muscles and joints. In fact, stretching loosens tight muscles, and this helps the muscles relax. Stretching also increases blood flow to various areas of the body and triggers the brain to release natural chemicals (i.e., endorphins) that make the body feel tranquil.

Warm bath: A warm bath provides both tactile and proprioceptive input and generally brings in a sense of calm. To make the bath more comfortable, you may want to suggest adding a bath pillow or fragrances such as a bath bomb. Many of these types of products are made organically and without chemicals and can be found online or in local shops. Finally, adults and children alike may find lower light during bathing more soothing. When working with parents and children, avoid the use of burning candles, but rather use battery operated candles and/or light sources.

Yoga: Yoga is a combination of many of these activities and is also an excellent form of exercise depending on what level one practices. As yoga has become more and more popular, yoga for young children is available both at yoga studios and gyms as well as online in the form of live and prerecorded classes. Yoga can also be a fun family activity and may also be an exercise program for adolescents.

A Note on Meditation: Numerous individuals have told me that therapists have suggested meditation and/or muscle relaxation techniques. However, I find that it is very difficult for people with misophonia to meditate or use muscle relaxation techniques because we are always distracted by sound, and our bodies are always in overdrive. Yet, with the body moving in yoga, the senses work differently, the attention systems work differently, and success is achievable. Meditation is wonderful, but I have always said that it is for the very well-regulated. People with misophonia need more sensory input and more movement.

Other Sensible Activities

Walking Outside

The outdoors is also a wonderful place for persons with misophonia—think simply of acoustics. If one is inside at a kitchen table, sound is not being absorbed. Outside, however, sound dissipates, which is why this is an effective activity. It is practical to suggest to your client that they use sound-absorbing materials in the home such as curtains, rugs, pillows, and so forth. Although this is not a cure-all, it can help a little, and a little goes a long way with misophonia.

A Place in the House

If you are working with children and families, you may suggest the creation of a special place in the house. Often, this is also helpful to younger adolescents. The place in the home can have sensory-based activities and offer a calming environment in which children or young adolescents can go to help regulate. For example, children enjoy little tents and fortresses. Often, school-aged children like music, soft pillows, various kinds of squeeze toys and/or toys that engage the tactile and proprioceptive system.

Teenagers may like similar items in their space and may also enjoy books, music, or calming videos they can watch on their phone. Older adolescents and adults often need "their own space." Often, this is easily negotiated between couples and within families. However, other times, you may be called upon to assist.

Listening to Music

Music can be an excellent source of relaxation even for those with misophonia. As I think we all now know, people with misophonia don't hate sound itself, rather they are averse to very specific kinds of sounds. Enjoying music, however, isn't as simple as listening to what is typically thought of as calming. The body of work in music neuroscience and music therapy tells us very clearly that while there are some universals in terms of calming music, such as a slow, steady, heart-beat rhythm, personal choice is really the deciding factor. For example, we hear birds in a great deal of presumably calming music. No offense to our feathered friends, but the sounds of birds does not relax me, and in fact, they do the opposite. So, don't be surprised if your client doesn't like what others typically find relaxing. We are all different!

Music can also change nervous system arousal, mood, and can even affect motor systems (Tomaino, C., 2019). Therefore, I recommend you guide your client in finding different kinds of music for the purpose of calming the body and/or uplifting mood. For books on music therapy and how to use music for self-regulation, please see the work of Dr. Dorita S. Berger.

Using Calming Activities Proactively

Many people with misophonia experience anticipatory anxiety. That is, they become anxious when they know they may be faced with triggers. Although this is natural, anticipatory anxiety serves to elevate the sympathetic system. In other words, with anticipatory anxiety at work, the individual is going from *50 to 90* rather than *0 to 60*. You can help your client through psychoeducation by explaining this clearly. You may assist more specifically by helping your client to plan as much as possible. The idea of using physiological calming exercises before one goes into a potentially triggering situation seems obvious but is often overlooked by therapists and clients alike. While it is impossible to always predict when sounds and sights may be triggering, proactive planning certainly helps.

The Tricky Translation

The trick in using these strategies is to translate them into the misophonic moment. In other words, being swaddled in a warm blanket may be calming to me even as an adult, yet if I were sitting in a classroom or giving a presentation, it would be both untimely and a bit strange if I were to suddenly wrap myself in a weighted blanket. Certainly, I would not be able to jump into a warm bath! The following lists activities that help self-regulation based on the same principles but can be done in the moment. Again, these activities are not a cure-all, but each is a part of a toolbox that will ultimately give clients the ability to better manage misophonia. You will also find a copy of *Translational Activities (Worksheet #2)* at the end of the manual.

Translational Activities (Worksheet #2)
4 Square breathing
Fidget devices
Hand gripper
Hand massage using pressure points
Placing of palms together with pressure
Placing something heavy (coat or backpack) on lap
Soothing visual stimuli
Submerging your face in very cold water

Examples of Translational Activities

4 Square breathing. 4 square breathing is an exercise where individuals inhale their breath for the count of 4 seconds, then hold their breath for 4 seconds. Then, they exhale for 4 seconds and then hold the breath for 4 seconds again. If 4 seconds is too difficult, a person can do this using 2 or 3 second intervals. Repeat until calm. In fact, there are numerous versions of this technique, all of which can be found on YouTube.

Fidget devices. Fidget devices are common tools used for people with various issues and can be found in toy stores. Some fidget device examples are fidget spinners and puzzle cubes. These devices, however, might not be a choice tool for families who have multiple misophonic children since fidgeting is a common visual/movement trigger. However, they are excellent for releasing tension.

Hand gripper. Often used in physical therapy or for guitar/bass players, hand grippers are squeezed and create tension or pressure. They offer intense proprioceptive input and work on the same principle as a stress ball. Stress balls, however, simply do not supply enough resistance for most with misophonia. In using hand grippers, make sure parents know to supervise their children so that they don't incur an injury as this is not a toy. Also, I advise purchasing the kind with variable tension.

Hand massage using pressure points. Massages to the hands are a common way to provide input to the pressure points that activate physiological calming. Hand massaging can be done anywhere, anytime, without others noticing. It is an excellent alternative to the hand gripper as it does not involve any equipment. Again, it is important to remember that for those with misophonia, it takes more input into the muscles and joints to affect change. Instruct your client to adjust the pressure to which they feel the massage is most helpful.

Placing of palms together with pressure. In a similar manner, placing the palms together is an easy way to provide sensory input that is deescalating to a person with misophonia. Anyone can learn to do this with variable versions of pressure depending on personal preference.

Placing something heavy on lap. While any heavy object can be used, *weighted lap pads* are smaller, more readily available, and often useful for clients at home, work, or school. However, as an alternative, a backpack or a heavy book can also be used to provide significant pressure that provides calming input. Adolescents and adults are likely to prefer these items as they are less obvious to use in school or in the workplace.

Soothing visual stimuli. Looking at something calming can also be very helpful. Examples of soothing visual stimuli that can be calming are paintings or artwork, fireplaces and crackling fires, aquariums, and running water such as streams and waterfalls. That which is personally soothing to a client is what usually works best. As a misophonia therapist, you can help assist clients to find what is soothing to them and guide them with how and when to integrate these activities to assist with self-regulation.

In addition, relaxing one's eye gaze tends to have a de-escalating impact on the entire body. Our eyes were meant to look far away, not close. You might want to try this yourself so that you can assist clients. It is worth mentioning because it is so easily done. Simply focus your eye gaze to a point in the distance, preferably as far away as possible. Then, reflect on how different your body feels. While this is not going to decrease trigger sounds, when a client is stuck in a car, a classroom, or even in the office, this quick exercise can de-escalate the nervous system just enough to allow one to think about their response and/or possibly do a *system reset*.

Submerging your face in very cold water. Many people experience a calming response when diving into cold water. We can initiate this response by submerging the face in very cold water. When the brain thinks the individual is diving, the mammalian dive response is activated, and the parasympathetic system responds to slow down one's heart rate via stimulation of the vagus nerve[3]. Many people use this successfully for panic attacks, and it is also an efficient way to quickly reach homeostasis regarding misophonia reactivity. Obviously, if you are working with individuals with low base heart rates or cardiovascular conditions, clear this with their primary physician. (Godek & Freeman, 2021)

Resetting the System

I want to emphasize that all of these sensory-based activities reset the nervous system. Of course, resetting the nervous system is much easier to do in the absence of a trigger. With children and younger adolescents, we often see raised tempers and actual requests or demands for others to "stop making that noise." Alternatively, we may see a child covering their ears and crying. Older adolescents and adults may attempt to hold in their reactivity, may leave the room, may ask others to "stop chewing/slurping/etc.," or may simply sit in silence as they continue to feel overloaded.

In either case, the purpose of resetting the system is so that the individual can return to a situation with decreased sympathetic arousal using one of the proactive and/or in-the-moment activities.

Often, children and young adolescents especially do not want to leave the family room, for example. The most likely reasons are because the person doesn't have the strategies to calm down, is conflicted, or doesn't want to be alone because they are in an overwhelmed state. It is important to understand that this is not obstinate or controlling behavior, although it may appear that way at first. Regarding adults, they are often in situations, such as the workplace, where they are unable to leave without serious consequences. An adult may also be attempting to enjoy the company of their family. The context for children, adolescents, and adults is variable. However, the tenants are the same. Regulate the physiological first by resetting the system physiologically.

Summary

In this section, we have reviewed practical sensory-based and physiologically based strategies that help keep sympathetic nervous system arousal low in general. Yet, we must modify these activities to use them in the moment that a client is triggered. That is why I call it the tricky translation.

Both naturally relaxing activities and exercise, as well as the in-the-moment activities are important, and it is essential to understand the difference. As we move on to the next section, I will address where the R for reasoning, which is the use of cognitive skills, comes in. The reasoning skills are not any less important than the physiological, but they don't work until some physiological self-regulation is achieved.

5.

Weaving the Three Rs Together

Putting together the three Rs is somewhat of an art that requires unpacking the multifaceted misophonic response into more manageable pieces. We need to learn to shift amongst physiologically regulating activities and the other facets of coping skills. Remember, reasoning includes cognitive appraisal and reframing of thoughts, and reassurance means helping clients know that you are working together in a nonjudgmental, empathic, and non-authoritative manner.

Weaving the three Rs together is not necessarily a linear process or a one-size-fits-all approach. Instead, weaving in between regulation, reasoning, and reassurance is somewhat like sculpting. The more you can explain and reassure clients that this is the case, the more you will assuage their anxiety about the disorder. Remember to refer to examples of corresponding worksheets and reminders in text here and in full form later. There is no precise order in which to use the worksheets. They are meant as tools for you to use along with your clients as you assist them in charting their individualized course.

Helping Clients Understand and Visualize the Fight–Flight Response

As you already know, it is essential that you explain the idea of fight–flight to clients and/or assist clients to explain this process to their loved one (such as a child or partner with misophonia). Remember, it is the educative part of RRR that leads a person to understand what is happening to the body during misophonia reactivity. Here is an example of a simple explanation:

The fight–flight response is a natural response in which the body prepares itself to deal with dangerous situations. When we are faced with a pressing danger, our bodies get us ready to fight the danger or escape from it.

The *Fight–Flight (Reminder Sheet B)* is useful for individuals with misophonia or parents of misophonic children to keep in their pockets. This is a quick reference guide that helps those either experiencing misophonia or who are assisting a loved one self-regulate.

Often, when one member of a couple is dysregulated, both become dysregulated. Similarly, one dysregulated member of a family easily dysregulates the whole family system. The fight–flight reminder sheet minimizes this dysregulation as it is a concrete tool that helps individuals focus energy on something productive rather than falling into the dysregulation trap. You might advise clients to make plenty of copies of this sheet so that they always have it on hand. You may also suggest to clients that they write their own version that reflects their own language or ways in which they would speak to their partner or child. Older children, adolescents, and adults can also write their own versions as well as illustrate them.

How Can I Explain Fight–Flight to Individuals of Different Ages?

Depending on a client's age, you will need to modify your description of this process. For a very young child, you might focus on how fight–flight makes different parts of the child's body feel. With an older child or adolescent, you can start by explaining how the brain sets off this process which is meant to get us ready to fight danger, yet the response can sometimes be set off by mistake. It may be helpful to ask adults and adolescents to self-generate times they were experiencing the fight-flight response. With younger children, it is often helpful to provide examples of times fight–flight may have been set off. For example, you may say to a child, "When you saw a bee in the backyard and you ran inside, that was fight–flight working the right way."

Explaining What this Means for Misophonia

Similarly, when working with misophonic individuals, it is imperative to connect sympathetic nervous system arousal, or the fight/flight response, to misophonia specifically. The following is an example of an efficacious way to make this connection for your clients:

When dealing with misophonia, we find that the brain misinterprets trigger sounds as dangerous or toxic. The brain then sets off the fight–flight response to protect the individual from the perceived danger. This response signals the misophonia sufferer to experience this reaction and the symptoms that come with it such as sweating, rapid heartbeat, and hormonal changes. These are the most frequent symptoms, and they can happen at inappropriate times.

Again, one needs to adjust these explanations according to developmental age and context.

Keeping Track of Triggers

Most individuals are aware of what their triggers are. However, I suggest using the *Keeping Track of Triggers* (*Worksheet #3*) for several reasons. This simple worksheet helps parents, adolescents, and adults to better understand the context of their triggers. This is not an exercise meant to be over-done or to encourage focusing on specific triggers. This exercise is only meant to help your client get an idea of the *what, when,* and *where* of triggers so that proactive planning, when possible, may be employed.

Keeping Track of Triggers (Worksheet #3)	
Sounds/visuals that bother misophonic person	When/where misophonic person experiences sound–visual

Separating the Physiological and the Emotional

As we unpack the misophonia response, we are almost constantly faced with having to help the individual separate the neurophysiological from the *emotion word*. Do your best to educate clients and emphasize the distinctions between reactivity and emotion, especially anger. Explain that the *sound* is making a client feel like running away, and if they cannot run away, then their body gets ready to fight. However, that feeling in the body is arguably not in and of itself an emotion.

Again, this process is an unnatural breaking down of a response that feels as though it is happening simultaneously. However, once a person understands the subtle similarities and differences between these interacting components, then there is room to work on them individually, thereby rendering a misophonic reaction much less daunting.

The *Misophonia Reaction (Worksheet #4)* is often a useful tool to help separate the physiological response from the idea of an emotion. This worksheet specifically helps to separate trigger sounds/visuals from feelings, thoughts, words, and actions. Again, using this worksheet and doing this exercise is not meant to be a stringent data mining process. The last thing a client needs is more stress. Instead, guide the client to use it as best they can as a source of information. This worksheet can be used repeatedly. For children, parents can engage their child in doing this activity by explaining that it is like a game. If a client is the parent of a young child, use the modified form that is less weighty at the beginning and move toward using the more comprehensive worksheet *Misophonic Reaction—Modified (Worksheet #5)*.

Misophonic Reaction (Worksheet #4)				
Sound or Visual	Physical Reaction	Emotion word	Thoughts	Actions

Misophonic Reaction—Modified (Worksheet #5)		
Sound/Visual Trigger	Physiological Response	Emotion Word

Monitoring Habituation

Monitoring regulation, or more specifically habituation, is another way to help clients both focus on the physiological and separate the physiological from the emotion words. Remember, habituation is the de-escalation of the sympathetic nervous system back to its neutral state and is what we are striving for.

In a sense, this next exercise is a little bit of biofeedback that one can experience at home without great expenditure of financial and other resources. Although these are very gross measures of the physiological system, one can use a heart monitor or a pulse monitor to track their baseline heart–pulse rate. Today, many people already have apps or devices that serve this purpose such as an Apple Watch or a FitBit.

Monitoring Habituation (Worksheet #6) is a way of recording how long it takes a client to habituate. However, the purpose of the exercise goes beyond just recording a measurement, I have found that many individuals are surprised to find that their body goes back to neutral much more quickly than they thought. That is why I always ask individuals to first guess how long they each think it will take for habituation to occur.

Often, people will say that it takes them a half hour to an hour to calm down. Yet, in reality, it requires much less time. Research has not vetted a typical time that sufferers of misophonia reach habituation after misophonia reactivity. However, clinically, I have seen a range from 30 seconds to 10 minutes. Notably, there is likely a large variation in terms of how long it takes for an individual to habituate, including the impact of other contextual circumstances. Like the other exercises, remember this is not meant to be a great work of science but rather it is something to help you help clients gain insight into misophonia and physiological functioning.

This is not an exercise that has to be repeated over and over again. Doing it even one time often sends the message. As long as your client takes less time to habituate then originally stated, this is often the “aha!” moment. It helps the individual with misophonia to feel a greater sense of self-efficacy in terms of this disorder.

There is also a more advanced version of this exercise that you can use with older children, adolescents, and adults. The more advanced exercise includes the original set of steps but adds one of the sensory-based techniques to see if that helps habituation happen more quickly. This is the exercise that often gets more mature individuals to buy into these coping-skills methods, thereby encouraging them to do the work.

Monitoring Habituation Instruction-Children & Parents (Reminder Sheet E)

Step 1: Instruct parents to ask their child to guess how long they think it takes them to calm down after being triggered.
Step 2: Most children guess that the process is much longer than it actually is. Once an individual is away from the offending stimulus, the de-escalating usually happens very quickly (in as little as 30 seconds).
Step 3: Suggest to parents that they take a baseline measurement of heart–pulse rate three times a day when their child is calm and in a neutral state, then average that.
Step 4: Instruct parents to move their child away from the offending stimulus when triggered and follow the rate of de-escalation.

- Instruct parents to measure the child's heart–pulse after triggered (although this is not what we are looking for).
- Continue to measure until the child is at baseline.
- Instruct parents to record the time it took for their child to reach baseline

Monitoring Habituation Instruction-Adults (Reminder Sheet F)

- **Step 1:** Ask your client to guess long they think it takes them to calm down after being triggered.
- **Step 2:** Many adults and adolescents guess that the process is much longer than it actually is. Often, habituation occurs in as little as 30 seconds when the individual is separated from the offending stimulus.
- **Step 3:** Suggest to your client that they take a baseline measurement of heart–pulse rate three times a day

when they are calm and in a neutral state, then average that.

- **Step 4:** Instruct your client to move away from the triggering stimulus and monitoring the rate of de-escalation.
- Instruct your client to measure heart–pulse after they are triggered
- Continue to measure until your client is at baseline
- Instruct client to record the time it took to reach baseline

Monitoring Habituation Recording Information (Worksheet #6)		
Time of trigger	Time back to baseline	Difference (time of habituation)
6:03	6:30	30 sec.

What if This Doesn't Work?

If your client reports that they are not habituating after being removed from the offending stimulus, then we know that there are other issues at play. For example, some individuals will continue to ruminate on the trigger sound or about the person from whom the sound emanated. In this case, suggest that the individual do exercises to quickly end rumination. What is the best way to end rumination in this case? The best way to end rumination involves getting out of the mind and into the body which can be through a sensory-based exercise that requires more strenuous movement or may be accomplished by listening to music, as some examples.

Please note that while there have been reports that obsessive compulsive and related disorders may occur with misophonia (Schröder et al., 2013) rumination about sounds/visuals, that does not necessarily indicate another disorder. Please take care not to jump to any conclusions as the research on this relationship is far from conclusive.

Movement in General: Releasing Adrenaline

You may have noticed that many of the sensory strategies involve movement. Movement is such a powerful tool in terms of de-escalating the sympathetic system that it warrants some extra attention. To see how powerful movement is, simply ask a client, or their parents, to note the difference in reactivity they experience when they are truly moving during an activity such as running, skateboarding, dancing, or otherwise.

I have asked many people with misophonia this question: "Do you have any misophonia reactivity when you are in a pool, running, or skateboarding?" Almost all have answered, "No." Often, this is a welcomed revelation as people realize that there are times in the day when reactivity is significantly decreased or even absent.

Finally, movement also demands attention. Remember preattention where the brain focuses on what is salient in the environment? Our preattention must go to our body's movement when we are navigating space. Our brains still scan for stimuli in the environment to warn us of a threat, but our preattention is also focused on the activity and not only on external sound and/or visual stimuli.

One technique I have found helpful is the *adrenaline release*. It may seem obvious, but to many with misophonia, it is not. Remember, those with misophonia are overwhelmed by this disorder and have likely read or heard a great deal of conflicting information. There are constructive ways to help the client learn how to release the adrenaline associated with fight–flight. We have talked about bringing in the parasympathetic system which brakes fight–flight. Some individuals also need to release the adrenaline that circulates the system when triggered.

The *Adrenaline Release (Reminder Sheet C)* provides positive ways for a person to do this.

Adrenaline Release (Reminder Sheet D)

Step 1: Review the activity with your client; explain the purpose so that it makes sense to the individual.
Step 2: Brainstorm with your client about which activities will serve

the purpose of adrenaline release. If the use of the word "adrenaline" is too elusive for a child, you can say, "to get out the bad energy," or whatever you think will communicate the concept best.

Step 3: For parents, you can suggest that the parent brainstorm a cue word that they will say to their child when they see escalation occurring. For adults, this is not necessarily needed as they are better able to self-monitor.

The goal of this exercise is to release the adrenaline but also to change negative valence to positive valence. Remember, valence is a qualifier to the sympathetic nervous system arousal level. The idea is to put into place an activity that a person can do in the moment at home, though it may not double as something they would do in public. Many of these activities may be modified, however, in public.

- Chair push-ups
- Jumping up and down in place
- Wall push-ups
- Jumping jacks
- Pretend to jump rope

Avoiding Triggers

Finally, it is extremely important to address trigger avoidance. Some psychologists have taken the stance that avoidance strategies are harmful. While living a life of complete avoidance of any potentially triggering situation is both impossible and deleterious to one's mental health, as practitioners, we must understand that avoidance relates to the *flight* part of fight-flight, and it is not necessarily a non-adaptive response regarding our defense system. Thus, our clients are fighting against what their brain is naturally telling them to do, and we must approach that with understanding and respect rather than formulating the opinion that *avoidance* is a personality trait rather than an adaptive part of our defense system.

Summary

The most important idea to remember in terms of weaving together RRR is that it is not a one-size-fits-all prescription. A therapist for misophonia is best when they hand the keys to the client (or to the family)—the keys to self-regulation.

In the next section, I address the typical issues that arise regarding family functioning and between couples in misophonia. Anyone who has a child or adolescent with misophonia knows that the family system is affected. Anyone who is navigating a relationship in which misophonia is involved knows how hard it can be. Yet, these situations can also be ameliorated.

6.
Family and Couple Dynamics

The dynamics related to misophonia are highly complex and would be best covered in a dedicated book. However, for now, it helps to go over the basics. As we do this, more worksheets are included to assist you. While there are similarities between adult and child misophonia sufferers, there are always nuances in relationships. Parent-child relationship dynamics are certainly different than spousal relationships (or coworker relationships)[4]. With that said, at the heart of successful coping skills development is the clinician's empathy for both misophonia suffers and their loved ones.

An individual with misophonia usually feels victimized by the overwhelming auditory and visual stimuli that is generated by those closest to them. A clinician is most effective when conveying understanding to the individual with misophonia and at the same time considering the feelings of family members and spouses, etc. Family members and partners often feel victimized by the misophonic individual's sudden unpredictable words or actions. If you are working with a family, adult individual, or couple, it generally helps to guide clients to help loved ones know that their feelings are valid and are also of concern while also acknowledging how difficult it is for the misophonic to live in a world where stimuli continually attacks them.

In misophonia, individuals almost always associate the sounds and visuals that trigger them with specific people. You will likely hear statements such as, “My sister is my worst trigger,” or, “My husband triggers me the worst.” Unfortunately, science has not established why the sounds and visuals generated by some people may be worse than those generated by others. Yet, it is important to remember that while misophonia entails orientation to person-based sounds, trigger sounds and visuals are not exclusive to *people sounds*, nor are they exclusive to mouth sounds. Sounds such as windshield wipers, pen clicking, beeping from electronic devices, and sometimes pets are among the various nonhuman sources that individuals with misophonia frequently describe as triggering (Brout et al., 2015; Jastreboff & Jastreboff, 2001).

Thus, the more you use a narrative that exemplifies people as triggers, the more you are supporting and solidifying a negative thinking pattern in your client. Simply changing the narrative may not change subconscious associations between trigger sounds/visuals and the people from whom they emanate. However, changing the conscious associations helps to remove the negative dynamic that often results from this pairing.

Separating Triggers for Children and Families

One of the easiest ways to help parents assist their child in separating trigger sounds and visuals from people is through *psychoeducation.* Try to help both parents and children understand that a particular noise—that is, their sibling’s whistling, not their sibling—upsets them. Adolescents often understand this, but it may be helpful to review these ideas. Sometimes, and most especially for younger children, explanation is not enough. This is something you can work with parents on assessing. For younger children, it is often helpful to go beyond verbally based psychoeducation by supplying a concrete example to children.

Separating Triggers from People (Worksheet #7a Children) will guide you through this exercise. The concept behind this activity is to create a concrete object for trigger sounds/visuals. By concrete, I mean something a child can hold in their hands.

Separating Triggers from People (Worksheet #7a Children)

- Guide parents to pick one or two specific situation-places related to corresponding triggers. For example, choose the kitchen and eating or the family room and sniffling, etc.
    - Note, the purpose of this is not to expose the child to trigger sounds purposely. Rather, this exercise should be used when a triggering moment naturally occurs.
- Parents can instruct the child draw a picture of a mouth and call it *Mr. Chewy* or *Ms. Breathing*. Card stock is preferable since it is more durable, but paper will do just fine. Parents can also use play dough or other types of clay to make these figurines.
    - I also like to use emoticon balls which are like stress balls but also have different emotions printed on them. They are usually available on Amazon.
- After the child has drawn and characterized triggers or the emoticon balls are available, guide parents to challenge their child to refrain from referring to family members as triggers (and that everyone in the family should also avoid this).
- If parents are using the emoticon balls, the child should

label them *Mr. Chewy, Ms. Sneezy*, etc.

- Then, when the family is at dinner, for example, and the child says something to a family member akin to, "You are triggering me," parents should ask the child to turn around so that they are not facing the person from whom the trigger is emanating.
- Parents should hand their child their drawing or emoticon balls (*Mr. Chewy*) and encourage them to talk to the sound or visual, saying something like, **"I can't stand you, *Mr. Chewy*."** It is essential that you guide parents to treat this like a game and an exercise, never as something punitive.
- Young children will usually enjoy this, and older children may think this is silly or embarrassing. However, encourage the family to try it just once. It is not the exercise itself that engenders change as much as it solidifies the point we are trying to make. It helps change the narrative, at least on a conscious level.
- If the child reacts positively, the family can do this more than once a day. However, they should not overuse the exercise as it tends to lose its efficacy as the novelty wears off. Again, the exercise is to shift cognition and consciously alter memory.

Helping Children and Siblings Understand-Family Negotiations

Adult sufferers may or may not have learned to effectively compromise prior to seeking help or may need more assistance to reach their goals. However, with children, the cognitive skills that underly the ability to compromise are less developed. Thus, it is important to guide children toward understanding that their reactivity, if focused on another person, is hurtful. It also helps if siblings are willing to learn about the disorder to understand its myths and realities as well as the personalization pitfalls. Whether you are working with a child or a family, you will be able to use your clinical experience to best judge how to express these dynamics.

Often, it helps for the family to make a rule that the misophonic child is expected to apologize when another family member's feelings have been hurt. This is especially important between siblings and helps preserve the relationship. Again, balance this out by guiding parents to verbalize how both children feel or by doing so in your office. For example, parents may say, "Your sister is very hurt because you gave her a dirty look," while also reminding the sibling that misophonia is not personal and that the family is working toward better misophonia management. Encourage parents to see this as a process and to reassure their children that they are getting help and the situation will improve.

Families can also work together by redoing the interaction. This gives everyone in the family a chance to modify their behavior in a calm environment. *"The Redo" (Reminder Sheet #D)* serves as a cue for this strategy. Make sure to tell your clients to only use this after the child with misophonia has habituated (or is calm). Yet, you don't want the family waiting too long as motivation may fade. Usually, giving the child just a few moments away from the offending stimulus allows for habituation and marks the time to start the exercise.

Parents may simply ask their family members to think about what happened and what they would each do differently to make the situation better. Then ask the family to speak aloud about their ideas. When everybody has a clear idea of what they want to try, they can proceed to do a redo of what occurred.

If you think it is best, you can certainly ask family members to recreate a typical situation from home in your office. However, the family should not recreate the trigger sound/visual nor the depths of emotional dynamics. This is not an exposure activity which is why a neutral sound should be utilized for the redo. We do not want the child with misophonia to become dysregulated. The aim is for the child/family to play out alternative actions while in homeostasis (neutral state). You can help keep the family regulated by using levity with this exercise to alleviate feelings of guilt or blame that various family members may be experiencing. You might suggest to the family that they do the redo as if they are acting in a comedic play.

Parents may find certain family members are uncooperative or may not want to participate in *the redo.* Yet, this is still an excellent exercise even if it doesn't involve everyone in the original situation. Remember, in the family systems theory, if one person in the family makes a positive change, the whole system alters for the better.

Separating Triggers for Adults and Couples

Although adults are more developed in their perspective taking skills than children are, misophonia can cause lapses in perspective in an otherwise typically developed adult. This often makes an individual with misophonia appear to lack understanding of that which their partner is experiencing. Again, an adult with misophonia may have spent decades feeling attacked by sounds they have associated with other people, especially via those closest to them (often now their partner or spouse). A wife may say, "My husband is my worst trigger." A boyfriend might say, "My girlfriend chews like an animal." A husband may say "I love my wife, but I don't know if I can live with her nose whistling—why does she have to do that?" By nature, some people are more empathic than others and can easily imagine how their partner may feel. Many adults with misophonia feel great shame and guilt regarding how they treat their partner, even though they attribute blame to them. *Separating Triggers from People (Worksheet # 7b)* will help you assist clients to approach this task.

The worksheet provided is a guide. However, your clinical

reasoning is very important in terms of when and how you bring this into RRR. As aforementioned, some clients will more easily be able to make this paradigm shift while others will have more difficulty. It is imperative to help clients be patient as this process involves memory processes that even neuroscientists struggle to illuminate.

Finally, keep in mind that although personality and cognitive style may affect how the individual does/does not attribute blame, 'inappropriate blame attribution' is not a sign of a personality disorder or personality style in misophonia. Blame attribution is often a consequence of feeling attacked by outside stimuli interfering with the individual's typical perspective taking abilities.

Separating Triggers from People (Worksheet #7b Adolescents and Adults)

- Before your client begins, instruct them to pick one or two specific situations–places related to corresponding triggers. For example, choose the kitchen and eating or the family room and sniffling, etc.
- Ask your client to draw a picture of a mouth, for example, and label it with the corresponding trigger. If possible, your adolescent or adult client should use card stock to make a wallet-sized reminder card. These cards are easiest for adults to conceal and use privately.
- After your client has drawn and characterized triggers, encourage them to refrain from referring to family members, spouses, or co-workers as triggers. Remember, psychoeducation is very important regarding coping skills development. Therefore, you should always explain the rationale behind any exercise.
- Guide your client to use their card to remind them that people alone are not intrinsically triggers.

Couple Negotiations

As we know, problems often occur when couples are experiencing everyday life activities such as eating dinner or simply watching television together at home. Other problems occur regarding lifestyle. Often, one member of the couple enjoys outings that the other does not due to the possibility of triggering situations. Whether you are working with one member of a couple or both, always abide by the idea of working on physiological regulation first. Yet, you will inevitably find yourself in the territory of couple negotiations. For example, your client may say, "My wife loves to go out to the movies, and I cannot deal with the popcorn crunching." What do you do then? Do you tell your client to accommodate his wife and try to control himself? Of course, the answer to that question is no. Remember, self-control and self-regulation are not the same. Any suggestion to your client that they simply should control their reactivity is antithetical to the most basic understanding of misophonia. Rather, you are helping your client develop self-regulation skills.

Conversely, guiding your client to automatically expect their significant other to accommodate them sets them up for great disappointment and excludes the humanity of the other individual. Therefore, we walk a fine line as clinicians in guiding the expectations of those with misophonia. *The Redo (Reminder Sheet #D)* can also be suggested to adult sufferers and their spouses if conflict is ensuing from misophonic moments.

Determining Necessary and Unnecessary Sounds

Below is an exercise that I always like to use for children, adolescents, and adults to help the individual think more comprehensively through the nature of their trigger sounds/visuals. Every now and then, I hear about a sibling using trigger sounds against their misophonic sibling. Certainly, this should not be allowed, nor should this be allowed between adult partners.

Although there are some noises that people make on purpose, there are also many noises that people must make that they cannot help. It assists clients to reason about which noises people *need to make* and which noises they *do not* need to make to shift perspective regarding blame attribution. You can do this in your office or guide clients (families or couples) to do this at home.

As a reminder, make sure to let your client know that they should only do this exercise when they are feeling very calm. As you are working with misophonic individuals, please remember that most are kind, empathic people who find themselves experiencing highly uncomfortable feelings and sensations that are not in sync with their personality. Please do not assume that your client, whether child, adolescent, or adult, lacks developmentally appropriate perspective taking or empathy. Rather, perspective taking is highly challenged in the misophonia moment as is cognition in general.

You will find the worksheet *Necessary, Unnecessary, & Habitual Sounds (Worksheet # 8)* in Section 8. Here, a client simply categorizes sounds and visuals into those that are necessary to sustain life, those that are not, and those that are habitual in nature. While I am using specific terms to express these concepts here, please feel free to use your own words that reflect the culture of your family.

As you go through this process with your clients, it becomes painfully obvious that most trigger sounds fall within the *necessary* category. Breathing and eating are the best examples of this. Other sounds/visuals are necessary because they are either spontaneous and cannot be helped but serve a physical comfort or health purpose. Examples of these are sneezing and throat-clearing. Sneezing is spontaneous, and throat-clearing is necessary to free obstructions. Of course, this isn't a perfect science, and some of these triggers, like throat-clearing, can also be habitual. Explain to clients that habitual sounds are often ones that others do without realizing it. For example, a parent may even explain to their child, "Your brother shakes his leg because he is nervous," or, "He needs some way of releasing his stress just like you." The process is the same within couple relationships.

You can use this list to make family or couple guidelines. For example, you might suggest that when a person produces necessary sounds/visuals, it is up to the individual to leave the room and do a nervous system reset or use other strategies. If someone in the family or a partner, for example, is tapping on their phone, you might consider this unnecessary and ask them simply to turn off the sound. Don't expect these guidelines to work perfectly. The point is to help your client develop a more positive narrative.

Necessary, Unnecessary, & Habitual Sounds (Worksheet #8)		
Necessary sounds/visuals	Unnecessary sounds/visuals	Habit sounds/visuals

Summary

It is important that a clinician is realistic when discussing with a client the extent to which the world will and will not be accommodating. You want clients to understand that some people may be willing to make accommodations to ease the burden of misophonia, while others, unfortunately, will not. While you may guide families and couples to work toward negotiations, remind them that even accommodations made by loved ones are not always possible. Sometimes it helps misophonic individuals to understand that misophonia is an invisible disorder that has no outward signs that cue others to modify their behavior.

7.
Conclusion

With misophonia, make sure your client understands that there are always going to be ups and downs and to expect variability across settings and at different times in their lives. Keep in mind that parents, teachers, and partners don't automatically understand this and may ask questions such as: "Why is so-and-so great during one class and not during another?" or, "Why can my husband eat with his friends but not with me?" Even people with misophonia are puzzled by this.

This confusing matter, unfortunately, begets parent or victim blaming. Research has not yet vetted this out, but most agree that these are mediating factors in misophonia:

- Poor sleep
- General health
- Mood
- Anxiety and stress

A clinician can easily become frustrated due to the challenges of working with misophonic individuals. Again, we are without a validated therapy now and must rely upon clinical reasoning and consultation with therapists across disciplines. RRR is a self-regulation approach to coping with misophonia that requires the integration of multiple skills that may call for additional education and possibly a paradigm shift for many.

We also face the unfortunate reality that we cannot make promises and claims to our clients. Clinicians certainly should not give the false impression that they can 'reduce triggers.' From the perspective of any individual with misophonia, unfounded claims are only harmful.

Given that we live in the age of the internet, we all see these unsubstantiated claims; they sometimes even sneak into peer-reviewed journals. I recall one of my graduate professors repeatedly asking her students, "Are you talking about research or *mesearch."* Unfortunately, there is a lot of *mesearch* out there posing as research. You likely have seen a myriad of therapists claiming they are successful in treating misophonia, and some of these over-stated declarations are made with the best intentions. Yet, we fail our clients if we do not discriminate amongst the research and statements about misophonia that we come across.

We can help our clients to cope through education, empathy, supportive listening, and self-regulation training. There is no easy-to-use treatment book that addresses this multifaceted disorder. Therefore, working with individuals with misophonia requires considerable professional dedication.

8.

Worksheets and Reminder Sheets

This section is available as a Word document on our website. The Word format allows you to edit the sheets with your own words.

Please go to www.misophoniaeducation.com/worksheets and enter the password "manualsheets" to download your copies for free as part of ownership of this manual. These worksheets are 8x10 and are standard letter-sized paper.

Reminder Sheets

Be Sensible (Reminder Sheet A)

- **Sight** (Vision)
- **Hearing** (Auditory)
- **Smell** (Olfactory)
- **Taste** (Gustatory)
- **Touch** (Tactile)
- **Interoception** (what we feel inside our bodies)
- **Vestibular** (sense of balance and rotation)
- **Proprioception** (sense of where our bodies our in space)

Fight–Flight (Reminder Sheet B)

What is the fight–flight response?

- The body's way of preparing itself to deal with dangerous situations when we are faced with a pressing danger; our bodies get us ready to fight the danger or escape it.

What does this mean for misophonia?

- When one is dealing with misophonia, the brain misinterprets trigger sounds as dangerous.
- The brain then sets off the fight–flight response to protect the individual from the perceived danger.
- This means that a misophonia sufferer will experience this reaction and the symptoms that come with it such as sweating, rapid heartbeat, and hormonal changes more frequently than others.

How can I explain fight–flight to my child?

- For a very young child, you might focus on how fight–flight makes different parts of your child's body feel.
- With an older child or adolescent, you can start to explain how the brain sets off this process which is meant to get us ready to fight danger but can sometimes be set off by mistake.
- It may be helpful to employ examples of times fight–flight should be set off (i.e., "When you saw a bee in the backyard and you ran inside, that was fight–flight working the right way.").
- Make your own reference sheet in your own words

based on how best to explain and remind your child what fight–flight is.

Adrenaline Release (Reminder Sheet C)

Step 1: Review the activity with your client; explain the purpose so that it makes sense to the individual.

Step 2: Brainstorm with your client about which activities will serve the purpose of adrenaline release. If the use of the word "adrenaline" is too elusive for a child, you can say, "to get out the bad energy," or whatever you think will communicate the concept best.

Step 3: For parents, you can suggest that the parent brainstorm a cue word that they will say to their child when they see escalation occurring. For adults, this is not necessarily needed as they are better able to self-monitor.

The goal of this exercise is to release the adrenaline but also to change negative valence to positive valence. Remember, valence is a qualifier to the sympathetic nervous system arousal level. The idea is to put in to place an activity that a person can do in the moment at home, though it may not double as something they would do in public. Many of these activities may be modified, however, in public. Some examples of these activities include but are not limited to:

- Chair push-ups
- Jumping up and down in place
- Wall push-ups
- Jumping jacks
- Pretend to jump rope

The Redo (Reminder Sheet D)

- Remember, when your client becomes dysregulated, the whole family, including spouses, may become dysregulated.
- We can call this group dysregulation.
- We also know from family systems that if one person in the family makes a change, the system itself changes.
- Therefore, if one person in the family makes a positive shift within the dysregulated dynamic, the whole family will benefit.
- If your client's family has regularly experienced group dysregulation, without placing blame on anyone, suggest that your client's family does a redo.
- Have your client or their parent simply ask family members to think about what happened and what they might do differently to make the situation better.
- Direct the group to speak aloud about their ideas.
- This is especially important for families that have very young children.
- When everybody has a clear idea of what they are going to try, proceed to do a redo of what occurred.
- The family or spouse should not recreate the trigger sound/visual. Instead, use a neutral sound for the redo. Your client may find certain family members are uncooperative or do not want to participate. Yet, this is still an excellent exercise even if it doesn't involve the whole family or all the family members who were part of the dysregulated group.

Monitoring Habituation Instruction-Children (Reminder Sheet E)

- Step 1: Ask your client to guess how long they think it takes them to calm down after being triggered.
- Step 2: Most parents, children, adolescents, and adults guess that the process is much longer than it is. Once an individual is away from the offending stimulus, the deescalating usually happens very quickly (in as little as 30 seconds).
- Step 3: Suggest to your client that they take a baseline measurement of heart–pulse rate three times a day when they (or their child) are calm and in a neutral state, then average that.
- Step 4: When triggered, instruct your client to move away from the offending stimulus and follow the rate of de-escalation.
- Instruct your client to measure heart–pulse after your client is triggered (although this is not what we are looking for).
- Continue to measure until your client is at baseline.
- Instruct client to record the time it took to reach baseline.

Monitoring Habituation Instruction-Adults (Reminder Sheet F)

- Step 1: Ask your client to guess how long they think it takes them to calm down after being triggered.
- Step 2: Most parents, children, and adolescents, and adults guess that the process is much longer than it is. Once an individual is away from the offending stimulus, the deescalating usually happens very quickly (in as little as 30 seconds).
- Step 3: Suggest to your client that they take a baseline measurement of heart–pulse rate three times a day when they are in calm and neutral state, then average that.
- Step 4: When triggered, instruct your client to move away from the offending stimulus and follow the rate of de-escalation.
- Instruct your client to measure heart–pulse after your client is triggered (although this is not what we are looking for).
- Continue to measure until your client is at baseline.
- Instruct client to record the time it took to reach baseline.

◆

Keeping Arousal Low at Home: Relaxing Activities–Everyday Practice (Worksheet #1)
Massage (foot rollers, hand rollers, etc.)
Rocking (or gliding) in chair
Rocking (or gliding) in chair with weighted blanket
Rolling on the floor or mat
Stretching
Taking a bath
Weighted blanket
Yoga
Write your own activities here.

Translational Activities (Worksheet #2)
4 Square breathing
Fidget devices
Hand gripper
Hand massage using pressure points
Placing of palms together with pressure
Placing something heavy (coat or backpack) on lap
Soothing visual stimuli
Write in your client's favorites here and add any ideas you have below.

Keeping Track of Triggers (Worksheet #3)	
Sounds/visuals that bother client	When/where client experiences sound–visual

Misophonic Reaction (Worksheet #4)				
Sound/visual	Physical reaction	Emotion word	Thoughts	Actions

Misophonic Reaction—Modified(Worksheet #5)		
Sound/visual trigger	Physiological response	Emotion word

Monitoring Habituation (Worksheet #6)

Time of trigger	Time back to baseline	Difference (time of habituation)
6:03	6:30	30 sec.

Separating Triggers from People (Worksheet #7a Children)

- Guide parents to pick one or two specific situations–places related to corresponding triggers. For example, choose the kitchen and eating or the family room and sniffling, etc.
- Note, the purpose of this is not to expose the child to trigger sounds purposely. Rather this is an exercise that should be done in the misophonic moment.
- Parents can instruct the child to draw a picture of a mouth and call it *Mr. Chewy* or *Ms. Breathing*. Card stock is preferable since it is more durable, but paper will do just fine. Parents can also use play dough or other types of clay to make these figurines.
- I also like to use emoticon balls which are like stress balls but also have different emotions printed on them. They are usually available on Amazon.
- After the child has drawn and characterized triggers or the emoticon balls are available, guide parents to challenge their child to refrain from referring to family members as triggers, and that it is important for everyone in the family to do the same.
- If parents are using the emoticon balls, the child should label them *Mr. Chewy, Ms. Sneezy*, etc.
- Then, when the family is at dinner, for example, and the child says something to a family member akin to, "You are triggering me," parents should ask the child turn around so that they are not facing the person from whom the trigger is emanating.
- Parents should hand their child their drawing or emoticon balls (*Mr. Chewy*) and encourage them to talk to the sound or visual, saying something like, **"I can't**

stand you, *Mr. Chewy*." It is essential that you guide parents to treat this like a game and an exercise, never as something punitive.

- Young children will usually enjoy this, and older children may think this is silly or embarrassing. However, encourage the family to try it just once. It is not the exercise itself that engenders change as much as it solidifies the point we are trying to make. It helps change the narrative, at least on a conscious level.
- If the child reacts positively, the family can do this more than once a day. For example, you might try it at two meals or three. However, they should not overuse the exercise as it tends to lose its efficacy as the novelty wears off. Again, the exercise is to shift cognition and consciously alter memory.

Separating Triggers from People (Worksheet #7b Adolescents and Adults)

- Before your client begins, instruct them to pick one or two specific situations–places related to corresponding triggers. For example, choose the kitchen and eating or the family room and sniffling, etc.
- Ask your client to draw a picture of a mouth, for example, and label it with the corresponding trigger. If possible, your adolescent or adult client should use card stock to make a wallet-sized reminder card. These cards are easiest for adults to conceal and use privately.
- After your client has drawn and characterized triggers, encourage them to refrain from referring to family members, spouses, or co-workers as triggers. Remember, psychoeducation is very important regarding coping skills development. Therefore, you should always explain the rationale behind any exercise.

Guide your client to use their card to remind them that people alone are not intrinsically triggers.

Necessary, Unnecessary, & Habitual Sounds (Worksheet #8)		
Necessary sounds/visuals	Unnecessary sounds/visuals	Habitual sounds/visuals

Made in the USA
Las Vegas, NV
11 March 2025

19380826R00055